The Pickleball Leadership Playbook for Educators

How Pickleball Builds Resilient, Connected Educators

Kaliym A. Islam, Ph.D.

© 2024 by Kaliym A. Islam

All rights reserved.

No part of this book may be reproduced or used in any manner without written permission of the copyright owner except for the use of brief quotations in a book review.

ISBN: 978-1-7369160-9-4

About Dr. K.
6

Also by Dr. K
7

Preface: From the Court to the Classroom – Why Leadership Matters
9

Chapter 1: Warming Up: Preparing Your Body and Mind for Success
12

Chapter 2: Foundations of Success – Leadership Skills for the Classroom
21

Chapter 3: Game Plan for the Classroom – Setting Goals and Strategies for Success
29

Chapter 4: Collaborative Play – Building Strong Teacher-Student Connections
35

Chapter 5: Quick Thinking in the Classroom – Adapting to Change with Confidence
43

Chapter 6: Teaching with Purpose – Strategic Decision-Making for Educators
50

Chapter 7: Trust on the Team – Building Resilience in Educational Communities
57

Chapter 8: Reflect, Revise, and Recommit – The Leadership Journey of an Educator
64

Chapter 9: Leading Beyond the Classroom – Inspiring Leadership in Education
72

Glossary of Pickleball Terms For Educators
78

Appendix 1: Summary of Research Study
81

Appendix 2: SMART Goal-Setting Worksheet
85

Appendix 3: Leadership Action Plan
87

Appendix 4: Classroom and Team-Building Activities
89

Appendix 5: Pickleball Leadership Drills
93

Appendix 6: Inspirational Leadership Quotes
98

Appendix 7: Professional Development Resources
101

Appendix 8: Articles and Journals
103

Appendix 9: Websites and Online Tools
104

Appendix 10: Online Courses and Workshops
105

Appendix 11: Pickleball Resources for Educators
106

Appendix 12: Parent and Community Engagement Toolkit
107

Appendix 13: Event Planning Template
109

Appendix 14: Strategies for Building Community Engagement
112

Appendix 15: Sample Scripts for Parent Communication
113

Appendix 16: Leadership Challenges and Scenarios
116

Appendix 17: Journaling Prompts for Self-Reflection
122

Acknowledgments and Further Support
125

About Dr. K.

Dr. Kaliym Islam, affectionately known as "Dr. K.," is an accomplished leadership expert, author, and educator with a passion for connecting sports and leadership. As the author of Pickleball Leadership: Lessons from the Court to the Boardroom and The Pickleball Leadership Playbook for Remote Teams, Dr. K. has inspired leaders across industries to embrace innovative strategies for managing teams in today's evolving workplace.

Dr. K. combines academic research with practical insights to help organizations and individuals thrive. When he's not mentoring leaders or writing, you can find him on the pickleball court, turning game strategies into winning leadership principles.

Also by Dr. K

The Pickleball Leadership Playbook For Remote Teams

Pickleball Leadership: Lessons From The Court to the Boardroom

The 12 Inch Rule of Leadership

The Agile Leaders' Guide

Agile Methodology For Developing and Measuring Learning

Podcasting 101 For Trainers

Developing and Measuring Training The Six Sigma Way

Dedicated to Remi Korchemny the ultimate educator.

Preface: From the Court to the Classroom – Why Leadership Matters

When I first stepped onto a pickleball court, I wasn't looking for leadership lessons. Like many others, I was drawn to the game's simplicity, the thrill of competition, and the joy of playing with friends. But the more time I spent on the court, the more I realized that pickleball wasn't just a game—it was a masterclass in leadership.

Each rally taught me something new: how to communicate effectively with a partner, how to adapt to unexpected challenges, how to balance strategy with execution. And as someone deeply invested in education, I couldn't help but notice the parallels between what I was learning on the court and the qualities that make great educators.

Leadership in education, like pickleball, is all about the fundamentals. It's about having a clear vision, creating consistent routines, and building meaningful connections. It's about trust, adaptability, and resilience. But here's the thing no one hands you a playbook for leadership when you step into the classroom. Most of us learn through trial and error, often feeling overwhelmed or unprepared for the challenges we face.

That's why I wrote this book. I wanted to create the resource I wish I'd had when I started my journey as an educator and leader. A resource that combines practical tools, relatable stories, and research-backed insights to help you not only survive but thrive in your role as a leader.

Why Pickleball?

You might be wondering: why pickleball? Why not basketball, chess, or some other metaphor for leadership? The answer is simple—pickleball is for everyone. It's accessible, adaptable, and endlessly engaging, much like the leadership principles it embodies. Whether you're a seasoned player or have never picked up a paddle, the lessons from the court are universal, and they translate seamlessly to the classroom.

Pickleball teaches us to:

- Build trust with our teammates.

- Communicate clearly and consistently.

- Stay focused under pressure and adapt to challenges.

- Lead with purpose, even when the stakes are high.

These are the same skills we need as educators to inspire students, collaborate with colleagues, and create positive, lasting change in our schools and communities.

What You'll Gain from This Book

This book is more than a guide—it's a leadership playbook designed to empower educators at every level. Each chapter connects a core leadership principle with lessons from pickleball, providing you with actionable strategies you can implement immediately. You'll find:

- Stories from educators who've applied these principles to transform their classrooms.

- Practical drills and exercises inspired by pickleball to reinforce key leadership skills.

- Research-backed insights that show why these strategies work.

- But most importantly, you'll gain the confidence to lead with clarity, consistency, and connection—both on and off the court.

Why This Matters

The world of education is more challenging than ever. Teachers are juggling growing demands, shrinking resources, and a need to connect with students in meaningful ways. Leadership is no longer optional—it's essential. And yet, many of us don't see ourselves as leaders, or we're unsure how to take that first step.

This book is here to change that. It's here to remind you that leadership isn't about titles or authority—it's about showing up, every day, with purpose and heart. Whether you're leading a classroom, a team of educators, or an entire school, the principles in this book will guide you toward becoming the leader your community needs.

So, grab your paddle and step onto the court. The game of leadership is waiting, and it's one you're more than ready to win.

Chapter 1: Warming Up: Preparing Your Body and Mind for Success

"Preparation is the key to success—whether you're stepping onto the court or into a new challenge, warming up gets you ready to play your best game."

What You'll Learn in This Chapter

By the end of this chapter, you'll be able to:

- Perform effective warm-up exercises to prevent injury and prepare for pickleball drills.

- Apply the concept of "warming up" to leadership, ensuring mental readiness for challenges.

- Create a personal routine to start each day with energy, focus, and purpose.

Introduction: Warming Up – Preparing Your Body and Mind for Success

Let's be honest—how many times have you skipped warming up before a game? It's easy to do, right? You're eager to hit the court, grab your paddle, and start playing. But then, a few points in, your muscles feel tight, your shots are all over the place, and you're already thinking, *Why didn't I take five minutes to stretch?*

The same thing happens in leadership. How often do we dive headfirst into the day—emails piling up, students asking questions, meetings waiting—without taking a moment to get our minds ready? No warm-up, no plan, just straight into the chaos. And just like skipping that pre-game stretch, it can leave us feeling scattered, reactive, and maybe even a little overwhelmed.

Warming up isn't just for athletes; it's for leaders, too. Whether you're stepping onto a pickleball court or into your classroom, how you prepare matters. It's the difference between feeling stiff and off-balance versus stepping in ready, focused, and confident.

In this chapter, we're going to talk about the importance of warming up—both your body and your mind. I'll show you some simple stretches and light drills to keep you injury-free on the court, and we'll also dive into ways to mentally prepare for your day as a leader. Think of it as your "pre-game ritual" for success, whether you're serving up an ace or kicking off a new project at work.

So, let's take a deep breath, shake off the rush to jump straight in, and give ourselves a little time to warm up. Because when you're prepared—physically and mentally—you're unstoppable.

The Physical Warm-up

If there's one thing I've learned from playing pickleball (and life), it's this: a good warm-up can save you from a lot of pain later. Whether it's a pulled muscle, a misstep, or simply feeling off your game, skipping the physical warm-up is like asking for trouble. And let's be real—none of us need extra trouble, on or off the court.

A proper warm-up isn't just about preventing injuries (though that's a big part of it); it's about getting your body ready to move. It's about waking up your muscles, improving your range of motion, and getting your heart pumping so you're energized and focused. It's the foundation for a great game—and it works the same way for leadership.

Let's walk through a simple warm-up routine designed specifically for pickleball players (but, hey, feel free to use it before tackling any big leadership challenges too!).

Dynamic Stretches: Loosen Up and Get Moving

These stretches are all about movement. They'll help you loosen tight muscles, increase flexibility, and mimic the motions you'll use during the game. **Here's what to try:**

1. Arm Circles:
   - Extend your arms straight out to the sides.

- Slowly make small circles, gradually increasing the size.
  - Reverse the direction after 20 seconds.

Why It Matters: Loosens your shoulders for swings and volleys.

2. Side Lunges:

- Stand with your feet wide apart.
- Shift your weight to one side, bending your knee while keeping the other leg straight.
- Alternate sides for 8-10 reps.

Why It Matters: Stretches your legs and improves lateral movement (essential for those quick side-to-side dashes on the court).

3. Torso Twists:

- Stand with your feet shoulder-width apart and hands on your hips.
- Gently twist your torso to the left, then to the right.
- Repeat for 10 reps on each side.

Why It Matters: Loosens your core and back, helping with rotation during serves and returns.

Get the Blood Flowing: Light Cardio

Once your muscles are stretched, it's time to get your heart pumping. This doesn't mean running a marathon—it's just enough to wake up your body and get your energy flowing.

1. Jogging or Brisk Walking:

   - Jog or walk briskly around the court for 1-2 minutes.

Why It Matters: Increases circulation, warms up your muscles, and boosts your energy.

2. Quick Feet Drill:

- Stand in place with your feet shoulder-width apart.

- Quickly shuffle your feet for 20-30 seconds as if you're running in place.

Why It Matters: Prepares your legs for quick directional changes during gameplay.

3. Light Paddle Work:

Grab your paddle and bounce the ball lightly on it, keeping control as you move around.

Why It Matters*:* Gets your hand-eye coordination going while warming up your wrists and arms.

The Mental Warmup

Pickleball players know that warming up the body is only half the battle. The other half? Getting your mind in the right place. Whether you're on the court or stepping into a leadership role, your mindset is what sets the tone for everything that follows. Rushing in without focus or preparation is like stepping onto the court without your paddle—you're setting yourself up for unnecessary mistakes.

Leadership is no different. Your ability to lead with clarity, confidence, and composure depends on how well you prepare your mind. This section is about mental warm-ups—simple practices to help you stay present, focused, and ready for whatever comes your way.

Why Mental Preparation Matters

Imagine starting a pickleball game distracted—thinking about that argument you had earlier or worrying about your to-do list. Chances are, your performance would suffer. Similarly, when you start your day as a leader without mentally preparing, you're more likely to feel overwhelmed, make reactive decisions, or miss opportunities to connect with others.

A mental warm-up helps you:

- Focus your attention on what truly matters.

- Approach challenges with a calm, clear mind.

- Boost your confidence and energy for the tasks ahead.

- Transition smoothly into a leadership mindset, whether you're teaching, coaching, or solving problems.

The Leadership Pre-Game Routine

Here's a simple, step-by-step routine to mentally warm up before your day or a leadership challenge:

1. Pause and Breathe

    - Take 1-2 minutes to close your eyes, take deep breaths, and let your mind settle.

- Focus on your inhale and exhale, releasing any tension or distractions.

Why It Matters: Calms your nervous system and creates mental clarity.

2. Visualize Success

    - Picture yourself succeeding in your upcoming tasks. Imagine the smooth flow of a lesson, a productive meeting, or a meaningful interaction with a colleague or student.

Why It Matters: Boosts confidence and primes your brain for positive outcomes.

3. Set an Intention

Ask yourself: *What's my main goal today?* Write it down or say it out loud. For example:

- "Today, I will focus on connecting with my students."

- "I will stay calm and composed under pressure."

Why It Matters: Gives you a clear focus and purpose for your day.

4. Identify Challenges

Take a moment to think about potential obstacles or challenges. Ask yourself:

- What might go wrong?

- How will I handle it calmly and effectively?

Why It Matters: Prepares you to respond to setbacks proactively rather than reactively.

5. Reflect on Your Strengths

- Remind yourself of your skills, experience, and past successes. Give yourself credit for what you bring to the table.

Why It Matters: Reinforces a positive mindset and builds self-confidence.

Practical Mental Drills

Just like physical drills sharpen your skills on the court, mental drills keep your mind agile and focused. Here are a few to try:

1. Mindful Journaling

- Spend 5 minutes jotting down your thoughts, goals, and concerns for the day.
- End with a gratitude list—three things you're thankful for.

Why It Matters: Clears mental clutter and shifts your focus to positivity.

2. The "What's Next?" Game

Before starting a new task or transition, ask yourself: *What's the next right step?* For example:

> Before a class: How do I want students to feel when they enter?

> Before a meeting: What's the key point I need to communicate?

Why It Matters: Keeps you intentional and present.

3. Grounding Exercise

- Use your senses to ground yourself in the present moment:
- Name 3 things you see, 2 things you hear, and 1 thing you feel.

Why It Matters: Reduces anxiety and brings you back to focus.

How This Translates to Leadership

Warming up your mind isn't just for high-pressure moments; it's for every moment. Whether you're teaching a lesson, addressing a conflict, or planning a new initiative, starting with a clear, calm mind allows you to lead with confidence. A mental warm-up prepares you to:

- Make thoughtful decisions instead of impulsive reactions.

- Stay grounded under pressure, just like a pickleball player who stays composed during a tight rally.

- Connect with others by being fully present and engaged.

Think of it this way: if you don't take the time to mentally prepare, you're leaving your performance—and your leadership—to chance. But when you warm up your mind, you're setting the stage for intentional, focused, and impactful actions.

Connecting it Back to Pickleball

On the court, mental preparation might look like visualizing your serves or reminding yourself to stay patient during a rally. Off the court, it's about preparing your mind for leadership challenges. The key is the same: focus, intention, and a readiness to adapt.

So, before you step into the classroom, boardroom, or court, take a few moments to mentally warm up. It's not just preparation—it's the foundation for success.

Chapter 2: Foundations of Success – Leadership Skills for the Classroom

"A strong grip, steady stance, and balanced connection—these are the foundations of success on the court and in leadership."

What You'll Learn in This Chapter

By the end of this chapter, you'll be able to:

- Define your classroom vision, just as you would establish your grip in pickleball, to guide your leadership approach.

- Refine your routines for consistency, mimicking the importance of a balanced stance on the court.

- Strengthen connections with students, colleagues, and parents, just as you build trust and synergy with your doubles partner.

Introduction: Building the Basics Together

Hey educators who love pickleball and pickleball players who happen to be educators, let's talk about the basics. Just like on the court, where mastering the grip, stance, and posture determines success, being a great teacher or leader starts with a solid foundation. Success in any environment—whether it's a school or a pickleball match—comes down to mastering the fundamentals.

Think about your classroom. Is your foundation solid? Are you clear in your goals, steady in your routines, and intentional in building relationships? These three leadership basics—clarity, consistency, and connection—will shape how you manage your classroom, inspire your students, and collaborate with colleagues.

Like a doubles player mastering a strong stance to return a shot, great educators know that building a foundation doesn't happen overnight. But when you focus on the fundamentals, you set yourself (and your students) up for success.

The Pickleball Connection: Grip, Stance, and Balance

In pickleball:

- **Grip:** Controls your paddle, giving you precision and control.
- **Stance:** Keeps you balanced and ready for anything.
- **Balance:** Allows you to connect with the ball, the court, and your teammate.

In teaching:

- **Grip = Vision:** Your vision for your classroom inspires and guides your leadership.

- **Stance = Routines:** Your routines create stability, helping students know what to expect.

- **Balance = Relationships:** Your connections with students, parents, and colleagues drive trust and engagement.

The key takeaway? Just as players build confidence through strong fundamentals, educators can lead more effectively when they focus on vision, consistency, and connection.

Backed By Research

Research reveals that even foundational pickleball play contributes to decision-making under pressure and confidence-building. In pickleball, players learn to make quick yet intentional decisions when returning shots, building confidence as they refine their skills.

One study participant noted:

"Pickleball taught me to focus on small, consistent improvements, which helped me grow as a leader in unexpected ways."

Educators experience the same growth. Mastering routines, managing classroom dynamics, and achieving small wins—like reaching a disengaged student—build confidence and resilience over time. Whether you're refining your morning routines or strengthening communication, success begins with consistency in the fundamentals.

Educator-Specific Example: The Ms. Rivera Story

Ms. Rivera, a first-year math teacher, felt overwhelmed during her first month in the classroom. She knew her success depended on building a strong foundation, so she focused on three key areas:

1. **Grip = Vision:** Ms. Rivera created a vision statement: "Every student will feel confident and valued in this classroom." She displayed it prominently and referenced it often to keep herself grounded.

2. **Stance = Routines:** She established consistent daily structures, starting each class with a warm-up problem and ending with a student reflection question.

3. **Balance = Relationships:** She made it a priority to greet every student by name and offer words of encouragement throughout the day.

The Result? Within a few months, student participation improved by 30%, and parents noticed their children feeling more confident about math.

Takeaway: Small, intentional actions—like establishing clear goals and consistent routines—build the trust and structure needed for long-term success.

Ms. Rivera's success highlights the power of mastering foundational leadership skills: having a clear vision, creating consistent routines, and building meaningful connections. Just like in pickleball, the fundamentals are where leadership begins."

Now, let's take these concepts onto the court. Building a strong foundation in leadership begins with mastering the basics—just like on the pickleball court. The following drills will help you practice the fundamentals of grip, stance, and posture while reinforcing clarity, consistency, and connection as leadership principles.

Try It On the Court: Foundational Pickleball Drills

To connect foundational pickleball skills with leadership fundamentals, try these drills:

1. The Grip Drill: Paddle Control for Vision

- How to Conduct:
    1. Use the "handshake grip" to hold your paddle naturally.
    2. Practice bouncing the pickleball on your paddle 10–15 times without dropping it.
    3. Gradually move the paddle side to side to build control

Leadership Connection:

Your grip in pickleball represents your vision in the classroom. A strong grip gives you control on the court, just like a clear vision gives you direction as a leader. This drill reminds you to refine your goals and align your daily actions with your broader purpose.

2. Stance Drill: Balance and Consistency

- How to Conduct:

    1. Start in a ready position (feet shoulder-width apart, knees slightly bent).
    2. Have a partner toss the ball randomly within a short area.
    3. Focus on adjusting your position to receive the ball with balance and control.

Leadership Connection:

Just like a balanced stance keeps you ready for anything, consistent classroom routines give you stability to lead effectively.

3. Connection Drill: Partner Dink Exchange

- How to Conduct:

    - Partner up and stand near the kitchen line. Softly dink the ball back and forth, aiming to keep the rally going as long as possible.
    - Focus on gentle, controlled movements and clear communication.

Leadership Connection:

Trusting your partner and communicating during the rally mirrors the importance of building strong relationships in the classroom.

Checklist: Leadership Foundations at a Glance

Use this checklist daily to strengthen your foundational leadership skills, ensuring clarity in your vision, consistency in your routines, and meaningful connections with students and colleagues.

Area	Yes/No	Reflection Notes
I communicated my classroom vision clearly today		
I followed consistent routines to create stability		
I made at least one meaningful connection with a student		
I adjusted my teaching strategies as needed.		
I reflected on what worked and what didn't.		

Closing Thought: Build a Strong Foundation

In both pickleball and leadership, success starts with mastering the basics. When you focus on grip, stance, and balance—your vision, consistency, and connection—you build confidence, trust, and momentum.

Take a moment to reflect:

- What's one leadership fundamental you can focus on this week?

- How can small, consistent actions help you build a stronger foundation?

Step onto your "court"—your classroom—ready to lead with clarity and purpose. Because when the fundamentals are strong, everything else falls into place.

Chapter 3: Game Plan for the Classroom – Setting Goals and Strategies for Success

"A clear vision is like a well-planned serve—it sets the tone for everything that follows."

What You'll Learn in This Chapter

By the end of this chapter, you'll be able to:

- Develop a strategic game plan for your classroom, much like preparing a strategy for a competitive pickleball match.

- Set clear, actionable goals that motivate your team (students or colleagues).

- Communicate your vision and expectations with precision, ensuring everyone is aligned on the court and in the classroom.

Introduction: Success Begins with Strategy

Every great pickleball match starts with a strategy. You don't just hit the ball aimlessly—you plan, anticipate, and adjust as the game unfolds. The same is true in the classroom. Whether you're setting goals for the year, designing lesson plans, or leading a team, having a clear game plan is what sets successful educators apart.

As educators, we juggle endless demands—curriculum requirements, student needs, and professional growth. Without a strategy, it's easy to lose focus and feel overwhelmed. But when you plan intentionally, every decision moves you closer to your goals.

In this chapter, we'll connect pickleball strategy to classroom leadership. We'll explore goal-setting techniques, practical drills, and leadership strategies that help you stay intentional, focused, and ready to adapt—just like a skilled player on the court.

The Pickleball Connection: Crafting Your Game Plan

In pickleball:

- **Strategic Shots:** You aim to place shots where they'll have the most impact.

- **Anticipation:** You read your opponent's position and prepare your next move.

- **Adaptation:** You adjust your strategy based on what's happening in the game.

In the classroom:

- **Strategic Goals:** You design lessons and routines that drive student success.

- **Anticipation:** You identify challenges and plan ways to overcome them.

- **Adaptation:** You refine your strategies based on student progress and feedback.

The mindset is the same: success requires clarity, purpose, and adaptability.

Backed By Research

Research highlights how goal-setting and intentional strategy—both on and off the pickleball court—contribute to leadership success. Players who focus on placing intentional shots build confidence, improve performance, and adapt more effectively during matches.

In educational leadership, similar principles apply. When educators set clear, measurable goals, they create opportunities for intentional teaching and meaningful outcomes. As one participant noted:

"The precision I learned through pickleball taught me how to focus my energy on small, impactful actions instead of trying to do everything at once."

Educator-Specific Example: Mr. Lopez's Game Plan

Mr. Lopez, a middle school science teacher, realized his lessons felt disconnected. His students struggled to see the bigger picture, and engagement was inconsistent. He decided to take a more strategic approach to his teaching:

- **Set Clear Goals:** Mr. Lopez created a mission statement: "To inspire curiosity about science and build critical thinking skills." He broke this vision into specific, measurable goals for each unit.

- **Plan Strategic Actions:** He designed lessons that tied directly to his goals, adding hands-on experiments to boost engagement.

- **Anticipate Challenges:** He identified common student misunderstandings and created targeted review activities to address them.

Results: Student engagement increased, assessment scores improved by 20%, and Mr. Lopez felt more intentional and focused in his teaching.

Takeaway: A clear game plan helps you align your actions with your goals, turning challenges into opportunities for success.

Try It On the Court: Pickleball Drills for Strategic Thinking

Strategic thinking starts with setting clear goals and aligning your actions to achieve them. On the court, the ability to plan and execute precise shots mirrors the intentionality required in leadership. Let's explore drills that build precision and adaptability, helping you develop a strong game plan for success.

To reinforce the connection between classroom leadership and strategic goal-setting, try these practical pickleball drills:

1. The Target Drill: Precision and Goal Setting

- How to Conduct:

1. Place cones or markers at specific spots on the court.

2. Practice hitting shots that land precisely on these targets. Start with easy placements and gradually increase the difficulty.

Leadership Connection: Just as a precise shot requires focus and intention, setting clear, measurable goals ensures your classroom actions align with your vision.

2. The Rally Drill: Adapting Under Pressure

- How to Conduct:

  - Pair up with a partner and aim to maintain a consistent rally for as long as possible.

  - Gradually increase the speed or unpredictability of your shots to practice quick adjustments.

Leadership Connection:

This drill highlights the importance of flexibility and staying composed under pressure—essential skills for adapting to challenges in the classroom.

Checklist: Strategic Goal-Setting in Action

Use this checklist to develop and refine your classroom game plan:

Task	Yes/No	Reflection Notes
I set a clear objective for my lesson or unit.		
I created activities that align with my goals.		
I identified how I will measure student progress.		
I reflected on how the goals support my long-term classroom vision.		
I communicated the goals to my students clearly.		

Closing Thought: Lead with Intention

Success on the pickleball court starts with a thoughtful strategy—an intentional game plan that keeps you focused and adaptable. The same applies to your classroom leadership.

By setting clear goals, planning strategic actions, and staying flexible, you can tackle challenges with confidence and lead your students to success.

Chapter 4: Collaborative Play – Building Strong Teacher-Student Connections

"Trust is the invisible net that keeps your team connected, both on the court and in the classroom."

What You'll Learn in This Chapter

By the end of this chapter, you'll be able to:

- Foster trust within your team, just as doubles partners rely on each other to cover the court.

- Create a safe environment for open communication, collaboration, and risk-taking.

- Recognize and address challenges that may erode trust, ensuring your classroom operates as a unified team.

Introduction: Why Trust Matters

Collaboration is the key to a successful team, whether you're working with a colleague, leading a student group, or playing doubles in pickleball. Trust is what keeps the team on the same page and working towards a common goal.

Trust doesn't happen overnight. It's built through small, consistent actions: sharing responsibilities, communicating clearly, and supporting each other through mistakes. Just like doubles partners rely on each other during fast-paced games, educators can foster trust in the classroom through intentional, consistent efforts.

In this chapter, we'll explore how trust and communication play a crucial role in both pickleball and leadership. You'll also learn practical ways to build trust and collaboration using strategies inspired by the game.

The Pickleball Connection: Building Trust Through Play

In pickleball:

Shared Responsibility: Doubles partners share the court, dividing responsibilities and working together seamlessly.

Clear Communication: Players must call out shots, strategize, and make quick adjustments to keep the rally alive.

Recovery and Support: Trust is built when partners recover from mistakes together and stay focused on the next point.

In the classroom:

Shared Goals: Students and teachers work together to achieve academic and personal growth.

Transparent Communication: Clear expectations and feedback foster a collaborative culture.

Supportive Leadership: Teachers build trust by guiding students through challenges and celebrating their efforts.

Backed By Research

Research highlights that trust and Research highlights that trust and collaboration are essential components of successful leadership, both on the pickleball court and in educational settings. In pickleball doubles play, partners build trust by consistently showing up for each other, communicating effectively, and sharing responsibilities. This mutual reliance fosters stronger team dynamics and resilience.

As one study participant noted:

"Trust isn't about perfection—it's about showing up consistently, supporting your partner, and learning from mistakes."

In education, similar principles apply. Classrooms thrive when students and teachers collaborate with trust and clear communication. Studies show that classrooms with high levels of trust and mutual respect experience increased engagement, improved problem-solving, and stronger academic outcomes.

One key finding from the study emphasized the importance of "small moments of trust," such as recovering from mistakes together or providing encouragement after a misstep. These moments build a foundation of teamwork and create a positive environment for collaboration.

Educator-Specific Example: Ms. Patel's Collaborative Classroom

Ms. Patel, a high school English teacher, noticed her students were hesitant to collaborate during group projects. Trust was missing, and group dynamics often broke down. To address this, she implemented strategies inspired by collaborative play in pickleball:

Shared Responsibility: She assigned clear roles within groups, ensuring each student had a specific, valued contribution.

Clear Communication: She modeled how to give constructive feedback and encouraged students to express their ideas openly.

Recovery Together: She created low-stakes group activities where mistakes were celebrated as learning opportunities.

Results: Over time, students became more confident in sharing ideas and supporting each other. Classroom discussions grew richer, and group project outcomes improved significantly.

Takeaway: Just like in doubles pickleball, fostering trust and collaboration in the classroom requires intentionality and consistent effort.

Ms. Patel's classroom transformation highlights the power of shared goals, clear communication, and mutual trust. These principles aren't just essential for classroom leadership—they're also key to success on the pickleball court.

Try It On the Court: Pickleball Drills for Collaboration

Collaboration and trust are at the heart of both effective teams and strong classrooms. Just as doubles players rely on clear communication and shared responsibilities, these drills will help you practice the principles of trust and teamwork that are essential for leadership.

1. Call Your Shot Drill: Communicating Clearly

How to Conduct:

- Play a rally with your partner, but every time you hit the ball, you must clearly call out "mine" or "yours."

- Focus on consistent, loud communication to avoid confusion and missed shots.

Leadership Connection: Clear communication avoids misunderstandings and builds confidence within the team, both on the court and in the classroom.

2. Trust-Building Drill: Coverage and Support

How to Conduct:

- Partners stand side by side near the baseline. One player focuses on covering the left half of the court while the other covers the right.

- The goal is to trust your partner to cover their zone without overstepping or hesitating.

Leadership Connection: This drill mirrors the importance of shared responsibilities and trusting others to do their part—key elements of team collaboration.

Checklist: Building Trust in Your Classroom

Use this checklist to assess and strengthen trust and collaboration in your classroom:

Task	Yes/No	Reflection Notes
I have established clear expectations and communicated them to my students.		
I actively listen to my students and respond to their concerns with empathy.		
I demonstrate consistency in my actions and follow through on promises		
I have created opportunities for open dialogue in the classroom (e.g., class discussions, feedback sessions).		
I encourage students to communicate openly with each other in a respectful manner.		

Closing Thought: Trust is the Foundation

On the pickleball court and in the classroom, trust is what holds teams together. It's built through clear communication, shared responsibilities, and consistent support.

Take a moment to reflect:

- What's one small action you can take this week to build trust with your students or colleagues?

- How can you create an environment where collaboration thrives?

Remember, trust is built over time—one intentional action at a time. Whether you're rallying with a doubles partner or leading a classroom, collaboration starts with trust.

Chapter 5: Quick Thinking in the Classroom – Adapting to Change with Confidence

"Adaptability is your greatest strength—stay flexible, stay focused, and you'll handle whatever comes your way."

What You'll Learn in This Chapter

By the end of this chapter, you'll be able to:

- Develop strategies for quick thinking and adaptability, mirroring the fast-paced decision-making required on the pickleball court.

- Stay composed under pressure, turning classroom challenges into opportunities for growth.

- Anticipate potential disruptions and create proactive plans to address them with confidence.

- Build a flexible mindset that encourages resilience and creativity in both yourself and your students.

Introduction: Teaching in a Fast-Paced World

Let's face it—teaching is unpredictable. One moment, your lesson is running smoothly, and the next, the projector stops working, or a student asks a question you didn't anticipate. In moments like these, quick thinking and adaptability aren't just helpful—they're essential.

In pickleball, the game moves fast. Players must react quickly to unexpected shots and adapt their strategy on the fly. The same principles apply to teaching. Your ability to stay calm, adjust your approach, and make confident decisions can turn challenges into opportunities.

This chapter is all about helping you develop the flexibility and composure you need to thrive in the ever-changing world of education.

The Pickleball Connection: Reacting with Confidence

In pickleball:

- **Quick Reactions:** Players must anticipate shots and respond within seconds.

- **Strategic Adjustments:** Players adapt their game plans mid-match based on their opponent's strategy.

- **Staying Calm Under Pressure:** Composure allows players to focus on the next shot instead of dwelling on mistakes.

In the classroom:

- **Quick Reactions:** Teachers often face unplanned challenges, from tech issues to unexpected student needs.

- **Strategic Adjustments:** Educators must pivot lesson plans or teaching approaches to meet their students' needs.

- **Staying Calm Under Pressure:** Maintaining composure sets the tone for the class and models resilience for students.

Backed By Research

Research highlights that pickleball enhances adaptability and strategic thinking. Players learn to analyze their opponents' positions, anticipate plays, and make quick decisions about shot placement—all while staying composed under pressure.

For educators, similar skills are vital. Studies show that teachers who remain flexible and proactive in the face of challenges foster a more resilient and adaptable learning environment. As one participant in the study noted:

> *"The adaptability I developed through pickleball helped me stay focused and confident, even during unexpected classroom challenges."*

Educator-Specific Example: Mrs. Thompson's Pivot to Success

Mrs. Thompson, a 4th-grade teacher, planned a hands-on science experiment for her students. But when the materials delivery was delayed, she had to think quickly to keep her students engaged.

Here's how she adapted:

1. **Stayed Calm:** Mrs. Thompson took a deep breath and reminded herself that the goal was student engagement, not perfection.
2. **Pivoted with Purpose:** She improvised by using common classroom supplies to demonstrate the experiment's principles.
3. **Focused on Opportunities:** She turned the situation into a lesson on resourcefulness, encouraging students to brainstorm creative solutions.

Results:

Students remained engaged, and the improvised activity sparked new ideas for future lessons. Mrs. Thompson's quick thinking not only saved the day but also taught her students an important lesson in adaptability.

Takeaway: Flexibility and quick thinking can transform challenges into opportunities for creativity and growth.

Mrs. Thompson's experience shows us how adaptability can turn setbacks into opportunities for learning and growth. Just like on the pickleball court, the key is staying focused, flexible, and ready to adjust to the unexpected.

Now, let's take these concepts onto the court and explore how pickleball drills can help you build quick thinking and composure under pressure.

Try It On the Court: Pickleball Drills for Adaptability

Adaptability and quick thinking are essential for thriving in fast-paced, unpredictable environments—whether on the court or in the classroom. The following drills are designed to sharpen your ability to respond to challenges with composure and confidence, ensuring you stay focused and resilient under pressure.

1. Reaction Drill: Staying Present

- How to Conduct:

1. Have a partner stand at the net and hit shots to random areas of the court.
2. Focus on reacting quickly and positioning yourself to return each shot.
3. Gradually increase the speed and unpredictability of the shots to challenge yourself.

Leadership Connection: Quick reactions on the court mirror the ability to respond effectively to unexpected classroom challenges.

2. Anticipation Drill: Thinking Ahead

- How to Conduct:

1. Stand at the baseline with a partner who hits shots to different areas of the court.
2. Focus on reading their body language to anticipate the ball's direction.
3. Practice adjusting your position before the ball is hit.

Leadership Connection: Anticipating the next move fosters situational awareness, helping you plan and adapt proactively in the classroom.

Checklist: Building Adaptability in the Classroom

Use this checklist to build adaptability and composure in your teaching, ensuring you can handle challenges with confidence and flexibility.

Task	Yes/No	Reflection Notes
I remain calm and focused when unexpected situations arise.		
I practice mindfulness or breathing techniques to manage stress in high-pressure moments		
I have identified potential challenges that could arise during lessons or classroom activities.		
I regularly review and update my plans based on student needs or feedback.		
I remain flexible in my lesson pacing and content delivery without losing sight of my goals.		

Closing Thought: Adaptability is a Superpower

Adaptability is the key to thriving in both pickleball and education. When you stay calm, adjust your strategy, and embrace the unexpected, you create opportunities for growth and success.

Take a moment to reflect:

- What's one area where you can improve your adaptability this week?

- How can you model composure and resilience for your students?

Chapter 6: Teaching with Purpose – Strategic Decision-Making for Educators

"Every decision is a step toward success—plan your moves with purpose and precision."

What You'll Learn in This Chapter

By the end of this chapter, you'll be able to:

- Deliver messages clearly and effectively, much like a well-placed serve that sets the tone for the game.

- Adapt your communication style to different audiences, ensuring your message resonates with students, parents, and colleagues.

- Use active listening to strengthen relationships and foster understanding in your classroom or school community.

Introduction

Great leaders and educators don't just react—they plan. In pickleball, every shot is an opportunity to think ahead, anticipate your opponent's next move, and position yourself for success. Similarly, in education, teaching with purpose means making intentional decisions that align with your goals and values.

- Strategic decision-making allows you to:

- Focus your energy on what matters most.

- Adapt to challenges with clarity and composure.

Build stronger connections with students, parents, and colleagues through thoughtful communication.

This chapter explores how you can apply the principles of purposeful planning and decision-making from pickleball to your classroom and leadership journey.

The Pickleball Connection: Strategic Thinking in Action

On the pickleball court:

Planned Shots: A well-placed serve sets the tone for the match.

Adaptation: Players adjust their strategies to counter their opponent's moves.

Quick Decisions: In doubles, partners communicate effectively to avoid missed opportunities.

In the classroom:

Planned Lessons: Thoughtful planning ensures your lessons align with your goals.

Adaptation: Adjusting your approach based on student feedback fosters engagement and growth.

Clear Communication: Delivering clear messages and listening actively builds trust and understanding.

Backed By Research

Research shows that pickleball strengthens emotional intelligence (EI), which is critical for leadership success. Key findings include:

- **Impulse Control and Focus**: On the court, players learn to manage frustration and stay focused after mistakes. Similarly, leaders who regulate their emotions inspire confidence and maintain team morale.

- **Empathy and Collaboration:** Doubles play encourages players to understand their partner's perspective and provide support, mirroring effective teamwork in educational settings.

- **Proactive Thinking:** Strategic thinking in pickleball translates to purposeful decision-making in leadership, fostering clarity and resilience during challenges.

Educator Specific Example

Ms. Carter, a high school history teacher, often felt overwhelmed by the demands of covering her curriculum while keeping her students engaged. After reflecting on her approach, she decided to apply strategic decision-making to her teaching:

Define Clear Goals: Ms. Carter outlined her primary objectives for each unit, focusing on critical thinking and historical analysis.

Adapt Lessons Strategically: She incorporated current events to make history relatable, adjusting her plans based on student interest and feedback.

Communicate Purpose: At the start of each class, she shared her lesson's goals and encouraged students to ask questions that connected the material to their own lives.

Results:

- Student engagement increased, with more meaningful class discussions.
- Ms. Carter felt more confident and in control of her lessons.
- End-of-term assessments showed improved critical thinking skills across her class.

Ms. Carter's success demonstrates how strategic decision-making can transform classroom dynamics. By aligning actions with goals and staying adaptable, you can lead with purpose both in the classroom and on the court.

Let's explore how practical pickleball drills can help reinforce the principles of strategic thinking and decision-making.

Takeaway: Just as a pickleball player plans their shots with purpose, educators can align their decisions with clear goals to create impactful learning experiences.

Try It On the Court: Pickleball Drills for Strategic Thinking

Purposeful leadership means aligning your actions with your goals and communicating with clarity. The drills below will help you practice intentional decision-making, strategic planning, and effective communication to enhance your leadership impact on and off the court.

1. Placement Drill: Planning and Precision

• How to Conduct:

1. Place cones or markers on the court and practice hitting shots that land precisely in these areas.

2. Gradually increase the difficulty by moving the markers farther apart or adding movement.

Leadership Connection: Intentional shot placement mirrors the importance of aligning decisions with specific goals.

2. Rally Drill: Communication and Adaptation

• How to Conduct:

1. Partner up and aim to maintain a rally while calling out each shot's placement ("left," "center," "right").

2. Focus on clear communication and adapting to your partner's shots.

Leadership Connection: This drill reinforces the importance of clear communication and the ability to adjust strategies based on feedback.

Checklist: Strategic Decision Making in Action

Use this checklist to ensure your teaching decisions are intentional, goal-driven, and impactful.

Task	Yes/No	Reflection Notes
I have clearly defined my short-term and long-term classroom goals.		
I ensure that each lesson plan aligns with my overarching teaching objectives		
I have prepared alternative strategies to address these challenges.		
I reflected on how the goals support my long-term classroom vision.		
I consider the needs and strengths of my students when planning lessons or managing the classroom.		

Closing Thought: Lead With Purpose

Every decision you make in the classroom shapes your students' experiences and growth. By planning strategically, staying adaptable, and communicating with clarity, you create a positive impact that extends far beyond the lesson.

Take a moment to reflect:

- What's one decision you can make today to align your actions with your goals?

- How can you model intentionality and resilience for your students?

Step onto your "classroom court" with purpose and confidence. Just like in pickleball, every move you make is an opportunity to lead and inspire.

Chapter 7: Trust on the Team – Building Resilience in Educational Communities

"Every great leader knows the secret to success: bounce back stronger than you started."

What You'll Learn in This Chapter

By the end of this chapter, you'll be able to:

- Build resilience in yourself and your students, just as players rebound from tough losses on the court.

- Teach strategies for managing stress and setbacks in constructive ways.

- Use failures as learning opportunities to refine your leadership approach and inspire growth in others.

Introduction: Trust as the Foundation

Trust is the key to success in pickleball, whether you're playing doubles or in school. In doubles pickleball, you need to trust your partner to cover their area and make smart decisions under pressure. In education, the same thing applies—building trust among teachers, students, and parents creates a strong and collaborative community that can handle anything that comes its way. Trust doesn't just happen by chance. It's built through consistent actions, open communication, and mutual respect. This chapter will show you how lessons from pickleball can help strengthen relationships in your educational community and make you more resilient in the face of challenges.

The Pickleball Connection: Trust and Resilience in Action

In pickleball:

- **Mutual Reliance:** Teammates trust each other to fulfill their roles without hesitation.

- **Recovering Together**: When one player misses a shot, the team focuses on the next point instead of dwelling on mistakes.

- **Communication**: Clear signals and shared strategies prevent misunderstandings and build unity.

In the classroom:

Building Trust: Educators and students thrive in environments where they feel supported and valued.

Bouncing Back: Resilient communities recover from setbacks and learn from challenges.

Fostering Connection: Transparent communication strengthens relationships and reduces conflict.

Backed By Research

According to the research, trust is one of the most significant benefits of playing pickleball in group settings. The study highlights that collaborative play—such as in doubles matches—requires players to rely on one another for success. This reliance builds mutual trust as teammates learn to anticipate each other's actions, communicate clearly, and support one another during challenging plays."

A participant noted:

'Trust is earned when you see your partner consistently showing up for you on the court.'

This insight reflects a core leadership principle: trust is built through consistency, reliability, and shared experiences. Leaders who demonstrate dependability and create opportunities for collaboration foster stronger, more cohesive teams."

The journal findings further emphasize that small moments of trust—such as covering for a teammate's mistake or setting them up for success—build a foundation for greater teamwork. These experiences mirror the leadership process, where trust grows through shared responsibility and mutual accountability

Educator-Specific Example: Ms. Rivera's Resilient Classroom

Ms. Rivera, a middle school art teacher, faced a challenging year. Her students struggled with low morale after remote learning disrupted their routines. She decided to focus on rebuilding trust and resilience within her classroom:

1. **Consistency**: She established predictable routines to create a sense of stability.

2. **Open Communication**: She encouraged students to share their frustrations and ideas, modeling active listening and empathy.

3. **Reframing Setbacks**: She introduced a "fail-forward" mindset, celebrating mistakes as opportunities for creativity and growth.

Results:

- Student participation increased by 40% within two months.

- Parents reported that their children felt more motivated and supported.

- Ms. Rivera felt more confident and purposeful in her teaching.

Takeaway: Trust and resilience go hand in hand. By fostering open communication and embracing challenges, you can inspire confidence and growth in your educational community.

Ms. Rivera's story shows us the power of trust and resilience in creating a thriving classroom environment. Just like on the pickleball court, every challenge is an opportunity to strengthen connections and bounce back stronger.

Let's explore practical drills that bring these principles to life and help you build a more resilient educational team.

Try It On the Court: Pickleball Drills for Trust and Resilience

Trust and resilience are built through consistent actions and a shared commitment to improvement. These drills are designed to strengthen your ability to foster trust and recover from setbacks, whether you're leading on the court or in the classroom.

1. Trust Rally Drill: Strengthening Mutual Support

- How to Conduct:

1. Pair up with a teammate and practice a rally where each player focuses solely on their assigned area of the court.
2. Communicate as needed but avoid overstepping into your partner's zone.
3. After each rally, discuss what worked and where adjustments are needed.

Leadership Connection: This drill emphasizes relying on others to fulfill their roles, fostering collaboration and mutual respect in your team or classroom.

2. Bounce Back Drill: Learning from Mistakes

- How to Conduct:

1. Play a doubles game where each pair earns bonus points for recovering quickly from missed shots.

2. Focus on staying composed and encouraging your partner after errors.

Leadership Connection: This drill mirrors the importance of resilience in leadership—bouncing back from setbacks and maintaining a forward-focused mindset.

Checklist: Building Trust and Resilience in Your Classroom

Use this checklist to ensure you're constantly working with your students and fellow educators in a way that builds trust.

Task	Yes/No	Reflection Notes
I communicate openly and honestly with my team.		
I encourage group projects that require shared responsibilities.		
I identified how I will measure student progress.		
I ensure everyone knows how their role contributes to the bigger picture.		
I regularly acknowledge student successes and efforts.		

Closing Thoughts: Stronger Together

Trust and resilience are the keys to great leadership, whether you're on the pickleball court or in the classroom. By building these qualities, you create a supportive environment where everyone feels brave enough to take risks, learn from their mistakes, and succeed.

Take a moment to reflect:

- How can you build more trust in your classroom or team this week?

- What strategies can you use to help your students or colleagues recover from setbacks?

Remember, every setback is an opportunity to build strength and connection. Step onto your "classroom court" with confidence, and lead your team to success—one point at a time.

Chapter 8: Reflect, Revise, and Recommit – The Leadership Journey of an Educator

"The most valuable lessons are found in reflection—on the court, in the classroom, and in life."

What You'll Learn in This Chapter

By the end of this chapter, you'll be able to:

- Develop a habit of reflective practice, analyzing your actions as thoughtfully as reviewing a game's key moments.

- Identify areas for personal growth and improvement, using reflection to refine your leadership approach.

- Encourage students to reflect on their own learning and behavior, fostering a growth mindset in your classroom.

- Use reflective tools to celebrate successes and apply lessons learned to future challenges.

Introduction: Leadership as a Journey

Leadership isn't a destination—it's a journey. On the pickleball court, every game teaches you something new. Maybe it's a shot you need to practice or a strategy you need to refine. In the same way, leadership in education is an ongoing process of reflection, growth, and recommitment.

Great educators embrace this journey. They take time to reflect on their successes and challenges, make adjustments where needed, and recommit to their purpose with renewed energy. This chapter is about embracing reflection and growth as essential parts of your leadership journey.

The Pickleball Connection: Reflecting to Improve

After every game, great pickleball players reflect on their performance. What worked well? What didn't? What adjustments can they make to improve for the next match? This cycle of reflection, revision, and recommitment is key to growth.

In education, the same process applies. By taking time to reflect on your teaching practices, revising your strategies, and recommitting to your goals, you continually grow as a leader. It's not about being perfect—it's about learning and improving every step of the way.

Backed By Research

Research underscores the importance of reflection in leadership and personal growth. In the pickleball study, participants noted that reflecting on their performance helped them identify strengths and areas for improvement, leading to measurable progress over time.

One participant stated:

"Every mistake on the court taught me something about my approach—whether it was my communication, my positioning, or my mindset."

Similarly, in education, reflective practice enables leaders to learn from their experiences, adapt to challenges, and foster a culture of growth and resilience. Reflection builds self-awareness and equips leaders to navigate complex situations with confidence.

Educator-Specific Example: Mrs. Taylor's Journey to Growth

Mrs. Taylor, a high school math teacher, struggled with time management. Her lessons often ran over, leaving little time for student questions. After reflecting on her practices, she realized she needed to adjust her pacing.

Here's how she did it:

Reflection: She started journaling at the end of each day, noting where she lost time and why.

Revision: She began setting timers for each part of her lesson to stay on track.

Recommitment: Each week, she reviewed her progress and recommitted to improving her time management skills.

Results:

- Within a few months, her lessons were more efficient.

- Students had more time to engage and ask questions.

- Mrs. Taylor felt more confident and prepared each day.

Takeaway: Reflection isn't just about looking back—it's about using what you've learned to move forward with purpose and clarity.

Mrs. Taylor's story shows us how reflection, revision, and recommitment can lead to meaningful growth. Let's explore how these principles can be reinforced through pickleball drills that emphasize self-assessment and continuous improvement."

Try It On the Court: Pickleball Drills for Reflection and Growth

Reflection and growth are essential for both leadership and personal development. The following drills will help you practice self-assessment and apply lessons learned to continuously improve your performance, ensuring you lead with purpose and confidence.

1. Post-Game Reflection Drill

- How to Conduct:

1. After a pickleball game, take 5 minutes to review your performance.

2. Identify one thing you did well, one area for improvement, and one adjustment to make in the next game.

3. Write down these reflections to track your progress over time.

Leadership Connection: Reflecting on your actions fosters self-awareness and continuous improvement, key traits for effective leadership.

2. Replay Drill: Learning from Feedback

How to Conduct:

1. Record yourself playing a game or rally.
2. Watch the recording to identify what worked well and what could be improved.
3. Practice the areas identified for improvement, focusing on actionable adjustments.

Leadership Connection: This drill highlights the importance of reviewing past actions and using feedback to refine your approach—a skill that's just as valuable in education as it is on the court.

Mini Case Study: Mrs. Taylor's Journey to Growth

Mrs. Taylor, a high school math teacher, struggled with time management. Her lessons often ran over, leaving little time for student questions. After reflecting on her practices, she realized she needed to adjust her pacing.

Here's how she did it:

- **Reflection:** She started journaling at the end of each day, noting where she lost time and why.

- **Revision:** She began setting timers for each part of her lesson to stay on track.

- **Recommitment:** Each week, she reviewed her progress and recommitted to improving her time management skills.

Within a few months, her lessons were more efficient, and her students had more time to engage and ask questions. Mrs. Taylor's willingness to reflect, revise, and recommit made all the difference.

Checklist: Structured Reflection for Educators and Leaders

Use this checklist to make sure you're constantly building on your successes and learning from your setbacks.

Task	Yes/No	Reflection Notes
I actively reflect on key decisions.		
I note the behaviors and decisions that led to those successes.		
I do lessons learned activities.		
I ask team members to share their reflections.		
I keep a journal or log to record key reflections and insights.		

Closing Thought: Embrace the Journey

Leadership isn't about having all the answers—it's about learning, growing, and staying committed to your purpose. By taking time to reflect on your journey, revising your strategies, and recommitting to your goals, you can lead with confidence and inspire those around you.

Take a moment to reflect:

- What's one area of your teaching or leadership that you'd like to improve?

- What's one small adjustment you could make to address it?

Remember, the journey is just as important as the destination. Step onto your "classroom court" with the mindset of a learner, and embrace every opportunity to grow.

Chapter 9: Leading Beyond the Classroom – Inspiring Leadership in Education

"True leadership extends beyond the classroom—it inspires, empowers, and uplifts communities."

What You'll Learn in This Chapter

By the end of this chapter, you'll be able to:

- Extend your leadership impact beyond the classroom, much like mentoring new players on the pickleball court.

- Inspire and influence colleagues, parents, and the broader school community through your actions and ideas.

- Develop systems for continuous improvement, ensuring your leadership evolves to meet new challenges and opportunities.

Introduction

Great leadership doesn't stop at the boundaries of a classroom—it extends to the hallways, the school, and the wider community. Just like a skilled pickleball player contributes to the spirit and success of the whole game, an exceptional educator inspires leadership beyond their immediate environment.

This chapter focuses on how you can take the lessons of leadership from your classroom and apply them to a broader context. By modeling collaboration, strategic thinking, and resilience, you can inspire others to lead, creating a ripple effect that strengthens your school and community.

The Pickleball Connection: Inspiring Leadership on and Off the Court

In pickleball, the best players lead by example, mentoring newer players, communicating effectively with teammates, and demonstrating sportsmanship. This approach builds a stronger, more cohesive team and a supportive community.

Similarly, in education, inspiring leadership means:

Mentoring and Supporting Colleagues: Sharing your experiences to help others grow.

Engaging with Parents and the Community: Building partnerships that benefit students and schools.

Advocating for Positive Change: Using your influence to inspire collaboration and innovation.

Backed By Research

Research highlights that pickleball's leadership benefits are most impactful when players actively apply lessons beyond the court. Participants in the study shared how patience, focus, and strategic thinking developed during games enhanced their leadership abilities in professional and personal contexts.

For example, one participant reflected:

"The patience I learned while dinking helped me stay calm and focused during a high-stakes project at work."

The study also emphasized the importance of follow-up actions to sustain growth. Leaders who identify specific takeaways and commit to applying them in their teams experience greater long-term benefits. This reinforces the idea that leadership development is a continuous process of learning, reflection, and action specific.

Example: Mr. Harris's Community Impact

Mr. Harris, an elementary school teacher, noticed a lack of parent involvement in his school. He decided to lead an initiative to build stronger connections between families and educators.

Here's what he did:

1. Organized Community Events: He hosted a "Family Pickleball Night," inviting parents, teachers, and students to play and learn together.
2. Facilitated Open Communication: He set up regular forums for parents to share their concerns and ideas.

3. Collaborated with Colleagues: He worked with fellow teachers to create workshops on supporting student learning at home.

Results:

- Parent participation in school events increased by 50%.

- Teachers reported improved communication and collaboration with families.

- Mr. Harris felt more connected to his community and inspired others to take similar initiatives.

Takeaway: Leadership beyond the classroom starts with small actions that create meaningful connections.

Mr. Harris's story reminds us that leadership has the power to inspire and uplift entire communities. Let's explore pickleball-inspired strategies that can help you extend your leadership impact and create lasting change.

Try It On the Court: Pickleball Drills for Inspiring Leadership

Great leadership inspires and uplifts others, creating a ripple effect of positive change. These drills are designed to help you practice mentoring, collaboration, and communication, extending your leadership impact beyond the classroom and into your broader community

1. Team Play Drill: Adapting to Different Needs

- **How to Conduct:**

1. Form teams of mixed skill levels and play doubles matches. Rotate partners after each game.

2. Focus on encouraging and supporting your teammates, regardless of their experience level.

3. After each match, discuss how you adjusted your approach based on your partner's strengths and needs.

Leadership Connection: This drill highlights the importance of adapting your leadership style to different individuals and contexts, fostering collaboration and trust.

2. Ripple Effect Drill: Amplifying Positive Actions

• **How to Conduct:**

1. After each rally, players must give positive feedback to their partner.

2. Reflect on how encouragement impacts performance and team morale.

3. Practice translating this approach to broader team dynamics.

Leadership Connection: Small actions, like a word of encouragement, can inspire others and create a ripple effect of positivity and motivation in your school community.

Checklist: From Learning to Implementation

Task
Review recent reflections or learnings. List the top 3 takeaways.
Define clear, actionable steps for each takeaway.
Share your action plan with your team for input and buy-in.
Set specific benchmarks or metrics to evaluate success.
Regularly check progress and celebrate small wins along the way.
Reassess insights and refine your approach for the future.

Closing Thought: Leadership That Inspires

Leadership doesn't stop when the school day ends. By extending your impact beyond the classroom, you can inspire others to lead, creating a ripple effect of positive change in your school and community.

Take a moment to reflect:

- How can you lead by example and inspire others to take action?

- What's one step you can take this week to build stronger connections with your community?

Remember, every action you take has the potential to uplift and empower those around you. Step beyond your classroom with confidence and purpose—your leadership can make a lasting difference.

Glossary of Pickleball Terms For Educators

1. **Adaptability:** The ability to adjust strategies, approaches, or mindsets in response to changing circumstances or unforeseen challenges in leadership or education.

2. **Balance:** In pickleball, the ability to maintain physical stability on the court; in leadership, the equilibrium between personal priorities, professional goals, and relationships.

3. **Clarity:** The ability to articulate a clear vision or message, ensuring that goals and expectations are understood by students, colleagues, or team members.

4. **Collaboration:** Working together effectively with others, whether in a classroom, on a pickleball team, or within a professional environment.

5. **Consistency:** Maintaining steady and reliable routines, principles, and actions that build trust and dependability in leadership and education.

6. **Connection:** The ability to build meaningful relationships with others, fostering trust and understanding, whether with students, colleagues, or parents.

7. **Decision-Making:** The process of evaluating options and making informed choices, a key skill in both pickleball strategy and educational leadership.

8. **Dinking:** A soft, controlled shot in pickleball used to maintain precision and strategy during a game; metaphorically used to emphasize finesse in decision-making and relationship-building.

9. **Engagement:** The active participation and investment of students, colleagues, or team members in achieving shared goals or objectives.

10. **Emotional Intelligence (EI):** The ability to recognize, understand, and manage one's emotions and the emotions of others, critical for fostering positive relationships and effective leadership.

11. **Forehand:** A basic pickleball stroke made with the palm of the hand facing the direction of the ball's movement, symbolizing direct and intentional action in leadership.

12. **Leadership Fundamentals:** The essential skills, traits, and principles—such as clarity, consistency, and connection—that serve as the foundation for effective leadership.

13. **Quick Thinking:** The ability to make decisions rapidly and effectively under pressure, essential for responding to challenges in the classroom or on the pickleball court.

14. **Reflection:** The practice of analyzing past actions and outcomes to identify areas for growth and improvement in teaching or leadership.

15. **Resilience:** The capacity to recover quickly from difficulties and maintain a positive trajectory, whether in education or personal challenges.

16. **Serve:** The initial shot in a pickleball game that starts play; a metaphor for taking initiative in leadership and classroom interactions.

17. **SMART Goals:** A framework for goal-setting that ensures objectives are Specific, Measurable, Achievable, Relevant, and Time-bound, used in both leadership and education.

18. **Stance:** The position of the body in pickleball that enables balance and readiness; in leadership, it reflects the principles and values that ground one's actions.

19. **Strategic Thinking:** The ability to plan and execute actions with intentionality and foresight to achieve specific goals, critical for success in leadership and pickleball.

20. **Team Dynamics:** The interpersonal relationships and interactions that influence a group's performance, whether on a pickleball court or in an educational setting.

21. **Trust:** Confidence in the reliability, integrity, and competence of others, forming the foundation for collaboration and effective leadership.

22. **Vision:** A clear and compelling picture of a desired future state, guiding actions and decisions in leadership and education.

23. **Volley:** A pickleball shot made before the ball bounces; represents proactive engagement and taking initiative in leadership.

24. **Warm-Up Activity:** An exercise to prepare physically or mentally for an upcoming challenge, emphasizing the importance of readiness in education and pickleball.

Appendix 1: Summary of Research Study

Enhancing Leadership Development Through Serious Leisure: Insights From Pickleball

Authors: Dr. Kaliym A. Islam, Nicholas J. Scalzo, and Dene Williamson

Research Focus: Exploring the relationship between pickleball participation and leadership skill development.

Purpose of the Study

The study investigates how playing pickleball, as a form of *serious leisure*, contributes to enhancing leadership capabilities such as:

- Team dynamics and collaboration
- Decision-making under pressure
- Personal growth, confidence, and adaptability

By connecting leadership development theories with the serious leisure framework, the study examines whether participation in pickleball fosters measurable leadership competencies.

Methodology

- Mixed-Methods Approach:

- Quantitative: A leadership behavior survey involving 133 participants assessed self-reported leadership skills. Participants were divided into:

    - Non-players
    - Occasional players (1–7 times per year)
    - Frequent players (8+ times per year)

- Qualitative: Open-ended questions allowed participants to describe how pickleball influenced their leadership abilities, offering deeper insights into perceived leadership growth.

Key Areas Assessed:

Leadership behaviors, communication, emotional intelligence, adaptability, and team building.

Findings

1. **Quantitative Results:**

- While the correlation between playing frequency and leadership skills was not statistically significant, frequent players reported slightly higher leadership scores overall.

2. **Qualitative Themes:**

Participants shared significant personal and leadership growth through pickleball participation. The key themes included:

- **Improved Team Dynamics:** Pickleball, particularly doubles play, enhances trust, communication, and collaborative problem-solving.

- **Decision-Making Under Pressure:** Participants emphasized the importance of quick thinking, adaptability, and staying calm in high-pressure situations—traits that align with effective leadership.

- **Personal Growth and Confidence:** Players noted that overcoming challenges on the court (e.g., learning new strategies) improved their confidence and resilience, qualities vital for leadership success.

3. Serious Leisure Dynamics:

Pickleball aligns with the principles of serious leisure, emphasizing perseverance, skill mastery, community engagement, and personal fulfillment. These attributes provide a unique and enriching environment for leadership development.

Conclusion

While statistical data revealed a minimal correlation, the qualitative findings demonstrated that pickleball provides meaningful opportunities for leadership growth. By fostering teamwork, strategic thinking, and emotional intelligence, pickleball serves as a practical and engaging tool for leadership development.

The study concludes that serious leisure activities like pickleball can complement traditional leadership programs, offering an experiential and accessible pathway for personal and professional growth.

Key Implications

1. Pickleball can be integrated into leadership workshops and team-building initiatives.

2. Structured reflection on gameplay experiences enhances leadership learning.

3. Future research should explore pickleball's leadership impact on a larger, more diverse population.

Appendix 2: SMART Goal-Setting Worksheet

Goal:

1. Specific:

   - What exactly do you want to achieve?

   (Example: Increase student participation during class discussions.)

2. Measurable:

   - How will you measure progress or success?

   (Example: At least 80% of students will contribute to discussions three times per week.)

3. Achievable:

   - Is this goal realistic, given your resources and constraints?

   (Example: Provide prompts and assign roles to students to encourage participation.)

4. Relevant:

- Why does this goal matter? How does it align with your vision or priorities?

(Example: Engaging students fosters critical thinking and collaboration.)

5. Time-Bound:

- What is your timeline for achieving this goal?

(Example: Within the next four weeks.)

Appendix 3: Leadership Action Plan

1. Goal:

2. Current Situation:

Where are you starting from?

(Example: Only a few students are actively participating in discussions.)

3. Desired Outcome:

What do you want to achieve?

(Example: 80% of students participating in class discussions.)

5. Action Steps:

List the specific steps you'll take to achieve your goal.

(Example: Use engaging prompts to spark discussion;

Assign discussion roles to each student; Provide feedback to encourage participation.)

6. Timeline:

Set deadlines for each action step.

(Example: Assign roles by the end of this week; evaluate progress after two weeks.)

7. Resources Needed:

What tools, support, or materials do you need?

(Example: Discussion prompts, role cards, and a participation tracker.)

8. Evaluation:

How will you know you've succeeded?

(Example: Track student participation weekly and compare it to your goal.)

Appendix 4: Classroom and Team-Building Activities

1. Icebreaker Questions for Building Connections

Use these questions to foster meaningful conversations with students or colleagues and build rapport.

For Students:

- What's one thing you're really good at that others might not know about?
- If you could have any superpower, what would it be and why?
- What's the best book, movie, or show you've seen recently?
- What's one thing you're excited to learn this year?
- If you could design your dream classroom, what would it look like?

For Colleagues:

- What inspired you to become an educator?
- What's a favorite teaching moment that stands out to you?
- If you weren't in education, what career would you choose?
- What's the best advice you've ever received about teaching or leadership?
- If you could make one change to improve education, what would it be?

2. Collaborative Team-Building Exercises

Activity: The Leadership Web

Objective: Foster trust and demonstrate the interconnectedness of team members.

Materials Needed: A ball of string or yarn.

How to Play:

Sit or stand in a circle.

1. One person holds the ball of yarn, shares one thing they appreciate about another person in the group, and tosses the ball to them while holding onto the string.

2. Repeat until everyone has shared and the group has created a web of yarn.

3. Reflect on how each person's contributions strengthen the group and how everyone is interconnected.

Discussion Points:

- How does trust impact teamwork?
- What can we do to strengthen our connections with one another?

Activity: Tower of Collaboration

Objective: Demonstrate the importance of teamwork and clear communication.

Materials Needed:

- Marshmallows or small foam blocks.
- Toothpicks or straws.

How to Play:

1. Divide participants into small teams.
2. Each team has 10 minutes to build the tallest tower using the provided materials.
3. The only rule: Each team member must participate in the building process.

Discussion Points:

- What strategies worked well during this activity?
- How did the team communicate and share ideas?
- What challenges did you face, and how did you overcome them?

Activity: The Gratitude Circle

Objective: Strengthen team morale and recognize contributions.

How to Play:

1. Gather participants in a circle.
2. One person starts by saying, "I appreciate [name] because [specific reason]."
3. The next person shares their appreciation for someone else, and so on until everyone has spoken.

Discussion Points:

- How does recognizing others' contributions impact the team dynamic?

- How can we incorporate gratitude into our daily work?

Appendix 5: Pickleball Leadership Drills

This section consolidates all the pickleball drills from the book, providing clear instructions and the corresponding leadership connections. These drills can be used as quick references for practice and reflection.

1. Grip Drill

How to Conduct:

1. Stand on the pickleball court with your paddle and ball.
2. Practice holding the paddle with a relaxed yet firm grip, focusing on proper hand placement (continental grip).
3. Bounce the ball on the paddle to maintain control and test your grip's stability.
4. Repeat for 5 minutes, adjusting your grip as needed.

Leadership Connection:

Your grip represents your vision. Just as a strong grip ensures control on the court, a clear vision provides direction in leadership. This drill emphasizes the importance of refining and aligning your goals to maintain focus and consistency.

2. Stance Drill

How to Conduct:

1. Stand in the ready position with knees slightly bent, feet shoulder-width apart, and weight balanced on the balls of your feet.

2. Shuffle side-to-side along the baseline, maintaining your stance and balance.

3. Practice returning balls from different angles while keeping your stance steady.

4. Repeat for 10 minutes, focusing on balance and fluidity.

Leadership Connection:

A balanced stance ensures stability on the court. In leadership, consistency provides a similar foundation for success, creating an environment where others can rely on you to lead with steadiness and confidence.

3. Communication Drill

How to Conduct:

1. Pair up with a teammate and practice a volley rally.

2. During each volley, call out "Mine!" or "Yours!" to coordinate who will return the ball.

3. Gradually increase the pace while maintaining clear and consistent communication.

Leadership Connection:

This drill mirrors the importance of clear communication in leadership. Just as effective communication prevents errors on the court, it fosters collaboration and understanding in classrooms and teams.

4. Anticipation Drill

How to Conduct:

1. Stand at the baseline of the court with a partner.
2. Have your partner hit shots to random locations on the court.
3. Focus on reading their body language to anticipate the ball's direction and position yourself accordingly.

Leadership Connection:

Anticipation allows you to stay one step ahead on the court. In leadership, it's about foreseeing challenges and preparing for them. This drill sharpens your ability to think ahead and make proactive decisions.

5. Trust Rally Drill

How to Conduct:

1. Pair up with a teammate and practice a rally where each player focuses solely on their assigned area of the court.

2. Communicate as needed but avoid overstepping into your partner's zone.

3. After each rally, discuss what worked and where adjustments are needed.

Leadership Connection:

Trust is essential for both pickleball and leadership. This drill emphasizes relying on others to fulfill their roles, fostering collaboration and mutual respect within your team or classroom.

6. Target Practice Drill

How to Conduct:

1. Place cones or markers at specific spots on the court.

2. Practice hitting shots that target these spots, focusing on accuracy and control.

3. Gradually increase the difficulty by aiming for smaller targets or adding movement to your shots.

Leadership Connection:

This drill reinforces the importance of precision and goal-setting. Just as targeting specific areas on the court requires focus, setting clear and measurable goals ensures intentionality and impact in leadership.

7. Replay Drill

How to Conduct:

1. Record yourself playing a game or rally.

2. Watch the recording to identify what worked well and what could be improved.

3. Practice the areas identified for improvement, focusing on actionable adjustments.

Leadership Connection:

This drill highlights the importance of reflection and continuous improvement. In leadership, reviewing past decisions and outcomes helps you refine your strategies and grow from experience.

These drills are designed to enhance both your pickleball skills and your leadership abilities. By practicing them regularly, you'll develop the clarity, consistency, and connection needed to thrive on and off the court.

Appendix 6: Inspirational Leadership Quotes

These carefully curated quotes highlight themes of leadership, teamwork, resilience, and growth, all of which align with the principles taught in The Pickleball Leadership Playbook for Educators. Use these quotes to inspire yourself, your students, or your colleagues.

On Leadership

1. "Leadership is not about being in charge. It is about taking care of those in your charge." – Simon Sinek

2. "A leader is one who knows the way, goes the way, and shows the way." – John C. Maxwell

3. "The function of leadership is to produce more leaders, not more followers." – Ralph Nader

On Teamwork

1. "Coming together is a beginning, staying together is progress, and working together is success." – Henry Ford

2. "Alone we can do so little; together we can do so much." – Helen Keller

3. "Teamwork makes the dream work, but a vision becomes a nightmare when the leader has a big dream and a bad team." – John C. Maxwell

On Resilience

1. "Do not judge me by my success, judge me by how many times I fell down and got back up again." – Nelson Mandela

2. "Success is not final, failure is not fatal: It is the courage to continue that counts." – Winston Churchill

3. "It's not whether you get knocked down, it's whether you get up." – Vince Lombardi

On Growth and Learning

1. "Leadership and learning are indispensable to each other." – John F. Kennedy

2. "Live as if you were to die tomorrow. Learn as if you were to live forever." – Mahatma Gandhi

3. "The greatest leader is not necessarily the one who does the greatest things. They are the one that gets the people to do the greatest things." – Ronald Reagan

On Communication and Connection

1. "The most important thing in communication is hearing what isn't said." – Peter Drucker

2. "Good leaders inspire people to have confidence in their leader; great leaders inspire people to have confidence in themselves." – Eleanor Roosevelt

3. "In every interaction, remember: connection is more important than perfection." – Rachel Macy Stafford

On Vision and Purpose

1. "The best way to predict the future is to create it." – Peter Drucker

2. "Your vision will become clear only when you look into your heart. Who looks outside, dreams; who looks inside, awakens." – Carl Jung

3. "The two most important days in your life are the day you are born and the day you find out why." – Mark Twain

These quotes can be displayed in your classroom, shared during team meetings, or used as personal reminders to inspire and guide your leadership journey.

Appendix 7: Professional Development Resources

This section offers a curated list of resources to support educators in their leadership and teaching journeys. From books to articles and online tools, these resources align with the themes of The Pickleball Leadership Playbook for Educators and provide additional insights into leadership, classroom management, and team-building.

Books on Leadership and Education

"The Art of Leadership" by Max De Pree

- A timeless guide to understanding and practicing effective leadership.

"The Courage to Teach" by Parker J. Palmer

- Explores the inner life of teachers and the importance of authenticity in the classroom.

"Leaders Eat Last" by Simon Sinek

- A deep dive into creating trust and building strong, resilient teams.

"Teach Like a Champion 3.0" by Doug Lemov

- Practical techniques for building relationships and fostering engagement in the classroom.

"The Five Dysfunctions of a Team" by Patrick Lencioni

- Insights into overcoming barriers to effective teamwork and collaboration.

Appendix 8: Articles and Journals

"Trust in the Classroom: The Key to Student Engagement"

- Journal of Educational Leadership, 2023
- Discusses the importance of building trust to enhance student participation and motivation.

"The Power of Reflective Teaching"

- Educational Psychology Today, 2022
- Explores how self-reflection improves teaching practices and student outcomes.

"Building Resilience in School Communities"

- Journal of School Leadership, 2021
- Highlights strategies for fostering resilience among educators and students.

"The Role of Goal-Setting in Educational Leadership"

- Leadership Quarterly, 2022
- A comprehensive look at how setting clear goals drives success in schools.

Appendix 9: Websites and Online Tools

Edutopia (www.edutopia.org)

- Articles, videos, and tools to help educators integrate innovative practices and leadership strategies.

ASCD (Association for Supervision and Curriculum Development) (www.ascd.org)

- Resources for professional development, curriculum planning, and leadership growth.

Harvard Graduate School of Education's Usable Knowledge (www.gse.harvard.edu/usable-knowledge)

- Research-based insights and practical tools for educators.

The Learning Network by The New York Times (www.nytimes.com/section/learning)

- Activities, writing prompts, and resources for engaging students in current events and critical thinking.

Appendix 10: Online Courses and Workshops

"Foundations of Educational Leadership" (Coursera)

- An introductory course on the principles of leadership in education.

"Classroom Management for Effective Teaching" (edX)

- Strategies for creating a positive and productive learning environment.

"Building Effective Teams" (LinkedIn Learning)

- Learn how to foster collaboration and trust within teams.

"The Pickleball Leadership Workshop for Educators"

- Offered by Pickleball Leadership. Explore how pickleball drills and strategies can transform classroom leadership.

Appendix 11: Pickleball Resources for Educators

USA Pickleball (www.usapickleball.org)

- Information on rules, drills, and resources to incorporate pickleball into educational programs.

Pickleball Magazine (www.pickleballmagazine.com)

- Articles and tips to improve your game while connecting it to leadership.

Live 2 Pickleball (www.live2pickleball.com)

- Drills, equipment, and community events for all levels of players.

This collection of resources supports ongoing growth and provides tools for educators to strengthen their leadership, teaching, and teamwork.

Appendix 12: Parent and Community Engagement Toolkit

This toolkit provides practical resources and tips to help educators build stronger relationships with parents and engage the wider school community. By fostering open communication and collaboration, educators can create a supportive network that benefits students and enhances their leadership impact.

Communication Checklist

Use this checklist to maintain effective communication with parents and caregivers:

Initial Contact:

- Introduce yourself at the beginning of the school year with a friendly letter or email.
- Share your goals for the class and ways parents can support their child's learning.

Regular Updates:

- Send weekly or monthly newsletters with updates on classroom activities, upcoming events, and student achievements.
- **Use tools like ClassDojo or email to provide real-time updates.**

Personal Touchpoints:

- Make time for individual parent-teacher conferences.

- Reach out with positive feedback, not just concerns, to build trust and rapport.

Open Lines of Communication:

- Provide clear ways for parents to contact you (email, phone, office hours).

- Respond promptly to inquiries and concerns to show parents their input matters.

Appendix 13: Event Planning Template

Organizing events is a great way to engage parents and the community. Use this template to plan effectively:

Event Name:

Date:

Time:

Location:

Objective: What is the goal of this event? (e.g., fostering parent involvement, showcasing student work)

Target Audience: (e.g., parents, guardians, community members)

Activities/Agenda:

- Welcome speech

- Student presentations
- Interactive activities
- Closing remarks

Materials Needed:

- Flyers for promotion
- Supplies for activities
- Food and beverages (if applicable)

Volunteers Needed:

-
-

Promotion Plan:

- Email invitations
- Social media posts
- Flyers sent home with students

Evaluation:

- What went well?
- What could be improved for future events?

Appendix 14: Strategies for Building Community Engagement

Parent Workshops

- Host workshops on topics such as:
- Helping with homework.
- Understanding the curriculum.
- Building resilience in children.
- Open House Nights
- Create opportunities for parents to explore the classroom and see their child's work.

Community Partnerships

- Collaborate with local businesses, libraries, or organizations to provide resources or host events.
- Invite community leaders to speak to students about careers or life skills.

Celebration Days

- Plan events that celebrate student achievements, cultural diversity, or milestones (e.g., "Student Showcase Night" or "Multicultural Festival").

Appendix 15: Sample Scripts for Parent Communication

Positive Feedback:

"Hello [Parent's Name], I wanted to share how impressed I am with [Student's Name] this week. [He/She/They] did an excellent job on [specific activity], and I'm proud of the effort [he/she/they] is putting into [subject]. Keep up the great work!"

Addressing Concerns:

"Hello [Parent's Name], I'd like to discuss how we can work together to support [Student's Name] with [specific challenge]. Could we schedule a time to talk about strategies that might help?"

Event Invitation:

"Dear [Parent's Name], we're excited to invite you to [Event Name] on [date] at [location]. This event will [purpose of event], and we'd love to see you there. Please let me know if you have any questions!"

Ideas for Strengthening Parent-Teacher Relationships

Create a Parent-Teacher Advisory Board:

- Invite parents to share their perspectives and help shape classroom or school initiatives.

Student-Led Conferences:

- Allow students to present their progress and achievements to their parents, fostering pride and ownership.

Thank-You Notes:

- Send personalized notes to parents who volunteer or support your classroom in any way.

Tools and Resources for Communication

- ClassDojo: A communication app that allows teachers to share updates, photos, and announcements with parents.

- Remind: A messaging app for sending announcements and reminders.

- Canva: A free design tool for creating professional-looking newsletters, flyers, and event invitations.

- Google Forms: Collect feedback from parents or RSVP information for events easily.

This toolkit equips educators with actionable strategies and tools to strengthen relationships with parents and engage the broader school community.

Appendix 16: Leadership Challenges and Scenarios

This section includes real-world leadership challenges and scenarios to help educators practice decision-making, adaptability, and problem-solving. Each scenario is followed by guided reflection questions to encourage thoughtful responses and learning.

1. Scenario: Addressing Student Engagement

The Challenge:

Your students are disengaged during a lesson you've carefully planned. Despite your efforts, they seem uninterested and distracted.

Reflection Questions:

- How would you adjust your lesson plan in the moment to recapture their attention?

- What strategies could you use to make the lesson more interactive and relevant?

- How might you reflect on this experience to improve future lessons?

2. Scenario: Managing Conflict Among Colleagues

The Challenge:

Two of your colleagues are in conflict over a shared resource, and their tension is starting to affect the team's morale.

Reflection Questions:

- How would you approach each colleague to understand their perspectives?

- What steps could you take to mediate the situation and find a solution that benefits the team?

- How might you use this opportunity to strengthen team dynamics and trust?

3. Scenario: Navigating Unexpected Changes

The Challenge:

An unexpected schedule change disrupts your carefully planned day. You now have to cover for a colleague and adjust your lessons on the fly.

Reflection Questions:

- How would you prioritize your tasks to ensure the most critical needs are met?

- What strategies could you use to stay calm and adaptable in the moment?

- How might you prepare for similar situations in the future?

4. Scenario: Supporting a Struggling Student

The Challenge:

One of your students is falling behind academically and seems increasingly withdrawn. You're not sure what's causing the change in behavior.

Reflection Questions:

- What steps could you take to learn more about the student's situation?
- How might you involve parents, counselors, or other resources to support the student?
- What actions could you take to build trust and help the student feel more supported?

5. Scenario: Leading a School-Wide Initiative

The Challenge:

You've been asked to lead a school-wide initiative to improve parent engagement, but there's resistance from some colleagues who feel it's too much additional work.

Reflection Questions:

- How would you communicate the importance of the initiative and address concerns?

- What strategies could you use to build buy-in and encourage collaboration?

- How might you recognize and celebrate small wins to keep the team motivated?

6. Scenario: Giving Constructive Feedback

The Challenge:

You need to provide constructive feedback to a colleague who isn't meeting expectations, but you're worried about damaging your relationship.

Reflection Questions:

- How would you frame the conversation to ensure it's productive and supportive?

- What specific examples and suggestions could you offer to help your colleague improve?

- How might you follow up to reinforce progress and maintain trust?

7. Scenario: Balancing Competing Priorities

The Challenge:

You're juggling multiple responsibilities—lesson planning, meetings, and mentoring a new teacher. You're starting to feel overwhelmed and unsure how to manage it all.

Reflection Questions:

- How would you prioritize your tasks to ensure the most important ones are completed?

- What strategies could you use to delegate or streamline your workload?

- How might you set boundaries or seek support to prevent burnout?

8. Scenario: Inspiring a Culture of Collaboration

The Challenge:

Your team has become siloed, with little collaboration or communication across departments. You want to create a more cohesive and cooperative culture.

Reflection Questions:

- How would you start fostering connections and building trust among team members?

- What activities or initiatives could you implement to encourage collaboration?

- How might you model the behaviors you want to see in your team?

These scenarios are designed to encourage self-reflection, discussion, and skill-building. Use them individually or as part of team training to enhance leadership effectiveness. Let me know if you'd like more scenarios or adjustments,

Appendix 17: Journaling Prompts for Self-Reflection

This section offers journaling prompts to encourage educators to reflect on their leadership journey, identify areas for growth, and celebrate successes. These prompts can be used weekly, monthly, or whenever deeper reflection is needed.

Reflecting on Leadership Skills

1. What leadership skill have I improved the most recently, and how has it impacted my classroom or team?

2. What leadership skill do I feel needs the most attention right now?

3. How do I balance being both a teacher and a leader in my educational environment?

Celebrating Successes

What is one moment from this week that I am particularly proud of?

1. How have I positively influenced a student or colleague recently?

2. What accomplishment reminds me why I became an educator in the first place?

Learning from Challenges

1. What was the most difficult decision I had to make this week, and what did I learn from it?

2. How do I typically respond to challenges, and what could I do differently to improve?

3. What would I like to handle better the next time I face a similar situation?

Building Relationships

1. What steps have I taken recently to build stronger connections with my students?

2. How have I supported a colleague or parent this week?

3. What's one relationship I'd like to strengthen, and what action can I take to start?

Aligning with Vision and Purpose

1. What is my vision for my classroom or school community?

2. How are my daily actions aligning with this vision?

3. What inspires me most about my role as an educator?

Inspiring and Leading Others

1. How have I modeled the behaviors I want to see in my students or team?

2. What's one way I've encouraged collaboration or teamwork this week?

3. How can I inspire others to step into leadership roles within our community?

Fostering Growth and Resilience

1. What's one mistake I've made recently, and how have I grown from it?

2. How do I encourage growth and resilience in my students or colleagues?

3. What's one action I can take this week to practice self-care and recharge my energy?

Looking Ahead

1. What's one goal I want to focus on in the next month, and why is it important?

2. How can I prepare for potential challenges in the upcoming weeks?

3. What steps can I take to ensure I remain motivated and focused on my long-term vision?

These prompts are designed to help educators explore their leadership style, celebrate progress, and plan for future growth.

Acknowledgments and Further Support

To all the educators reading this book: thank you.

Your dedication to your students, your willingness to grow as leaders, and your efforts to create meaningful change in education are truly inspiring. This book exists because of educators like you who continuously strive to make a difference.

A special acknowledgment to the teachers who lead by example, the colleagues who collaborate selflessly, and the parents and community members who partner with educators to support student success. Together, we are building a brighter future for all learners.

Further Support and Resources

Stay Connected

- Visit www.pickleballleadership.com for additional resources, including free leadership templates, course offerings, and community discussions.

- Follow me on @thetrainingpro on X for tips, inspiration, and updates on future projects.

Join the Leadership Community

- Become a member of the Pickleball Leadership Network, where educators can share insights, collaborate on challenges, and celebrate successes.

- Sign up for the monthly newsletter to receive exclusive tools, articles, and strategies for educational leadership.

Workshops and Events

- Explore The Pickleball Leadership Workshop for Educators, a hands-on experience that combines leadership principles with pickleball strategies to enhance collaboration and resilience.

- Attend virtual and in-person sessions to connect with other educators and develop actionable skills.

Leadership Courses

Enroll in online courses, such as:

- Fundamentals of Leadership for Educators
- Building Trust and Resilience in Your School Community
- Pickleball-Inspired Team Building for Educators

Feedback and Collaboration

- Your input is invaluable. Share your feedback on this book or suggest topics for future editions at kaliym@pickleballleadership.com.

- Collaborate with me on workshops, school initiatives, or customized leadership programs tailored to your team.

Upcoming Books in the Series

- Look out for The Pickleball Leadership Playbook for Administrators and The Pickleball Leadership Playbook for Parents.

- Sign up to receive updates and sneak previews of new content.

Closing Message

Leadership is a journey, and you're never alone on the path. Whether you're working in your classroom, collaborating with your team, or inspiring change in your community, your impact matters.

Thank you for stepping into this role with courage, passion, and purpose. Keep leading, learning, and growing—and know that I'm here to support you every step of the way.

Warm regards,

Dr. K.

www.ingramcontent.com/pod-product-compliance
Lightning Source LLC
Chambersburg PA
CBHW070202100426
42743CB00013B/3019